FIRESIDE SERIES

Volume 2, No. 5

Ramtha

Who Are We Really?

Who Are We Really?
Revised Edition

Copyright © 2002, 2006 JZ Knight.

Cover design by Melissa Peizer

The contents of this publication are based on Ramtha Dialogues®, a series of magnetic tape and compact disc recordings registered with the United States Copyright Office, with permission from JZ Knight and JZK, Inc.

This work is based on the partial transcription of Ramtha Dialogues®, Tape 353, *In the Beginning — Level 1,* May 3-4, 1997. Copyright ℗ 1997 JZ Knight.

Ramtha®, Ramtha Dialogues®, C&E®, Consciousness & Energy℠, Fieldwork℠, The Tank®, Blue Body®, Twilight®, Torsion Process℠, Neighborhood Walk℠, Create Your Day℠, The Grid℠, and Become a Remarkable Life™ are trademarks and service marks of JZ Knight and are used with permission.

ISBN # 1-57873-067-8

JZK Publishing
A Division of JZK, Inc.

Ramtha's School of Enlightenment
P.O. Box 1210
Yelm, Washington 98597
360.458.5201
800.347.0439
www.ramtha.com
www.jzkpublishing.com

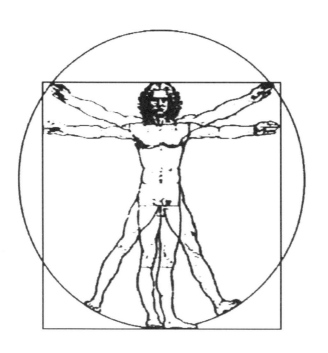

These series of teachings are designed for all the students of the Great Work who love the teachings of the Ram.

It is suggested that you create an ideal learning environment for study and contemplation.

Light your fireplace and get cozy. Prepare yourself. Open your mind to learn and be genius.

FOREWORD

The Fireside Series is an ongoing library of the hottest topics of interest taught by Ramtha. These series of teachings are designed for all the students of the Great Work who love the teachings of the Ram. This collection is also intended as a continuing learning tool for the students of Ramtha's School of Enlightenment and for everyone interested and familiar with Ramtha's teachings. In the last three decades Ramtha has continuously and methodically deepened and expanded his exposition of the nature of reality and its practical application through various disciplines. It is assumed by the publisher that the reader has attended a Beginning Retreat or workshop through Ramtha's School of Enlightenment or is at least familiar with Ramtha's instruction to his beginning class of students. This introductory information is found in *Ramtha: A Beginner's Guide to Creating Reality*, Third Ed. (Yelm: JZK Publishing, a division of JZK, Inc., 2004).

We have included in the Fireside Series a glossary of some of the basic concepts used by Ramtha so the reader can become familiarized with these teachings. We have also included a brief introduction of Ramtha by JZ Knight that describes how all this began for those who are unfamiliar with the story. Enjoy your learning and contemplation.

Contents

List of Figures

DON'T YOU KNOW YOU ARE GOD?

I salute you from the Lord God of my being to the Lord God of your being.

The salutation that we do when we come together we do in the name of God. And, yes, there is a God, but what is more important is that God interact with you and uplift your Spirit today, open your mind to what you are going to learn, open your soul that you accept the runners that are going to come to you, and all that happens to you that you will be uplifted.

So this is our prayer:

My beloved God,
Mysterious One,
that which gave me life
and holds my purpose,
of this day
I celebrate my life.
I desire my knowledge
to expand.
I desire my body
to be healed.
This I give permission to.
Of this day
I desire that my life
change,
that your purpose for my life
I may realize.
God bless my life.
So be it.
To life.

You have heard rumor I am Ramtha the Enlightened One. I have been for as long as I have known me. I am the entity that your relatives and friends have talked about. I am a teacher, most certainly, and I am real, according to your scientists.

I am here because many of my people a long, long time ago, before the narrow-mindedness of humanity really set in, had an opportunity to go on with their life after great conquests and their cherished retirement on a continent that was peaceful. Those people were my people. And yet where I went, there was nothing written in books and there was certainly no television. They never said you couldn't go there or you couldn't do this, and I finished my life here and went on.

There was no teacher that ever taught me how to do that except nature. I became an observer of nature and finally its lover, and I went on because there was nothing else to challenge me here. My people stayed because they wanted a life and they wanted to cultivate children and generations, create land and assets, and all of that. I told them before I left, "One day I will come back. And when you are ready to see where I went, after you have had many lifetimes and many bodies that you have worn to experience this, I will show you where I went and how to get there." Well, this is who I am.

I planned to come back here in a most ingenious manner because over time there has been a tremendous prejudice that you have incurred and carried with you through generations, and it sits in your soul. Two of the prejudices are, first, that God is only admissible to men — what a farce — and that women are less than men, thereby the kingdom of heaven is not given to them, lest it is given to them by the male gender.

God, today in your life, is always referred to as he. His only son was a he. And those neutered priests are "hims" that stand as interpreters between the impure woman and the holy of holies. Garbage, all of it. What we see, even in what you call the modern day, is that there is still a resistance to treating women other than assets or something to lay with in bed. You cannot know that which is if you are blocked by prejudices.

I came back here with an entity who in my lifetime very much wanted to go where I went and wanted to lead an army. Now that has been made manifest. And the army is much tougher than the one 35,000 years ago. What we march against here is closed-mindedness. It is not for the world. It is for those who want to come and learn about that.

What I am had nothing to do with my body any more than what you are has anything to do with your body. What I am is here as full-force consciousness in a female body. Those who have been around me for a while have no doubt in their mind that I was a man — none — but here is also the consciousness and the Spirit of myself working through a female body. This brain is a computer and I set my will at its subconscious in the back of its head and it operates the rest of the body.

When you look at me we can't say then altogether that God is a man or that God is a woman, but we can certainly say that God must be both and neither. Well, that is the message. You see, God has no affiliation with gender, has nothing to do with gender or a body, and has everything to do with personal opinion. It is what we call the spiritual self.

I came back and in a very common and simple woman brought about a great truth before it became fashionable. What I said was: Don't you know who you are? Don't you know you are God? And why would you think any different? And who say you are not? I tell you that you are. Then what must you do to realize that? You must become an individual. Indeed you do that by knowing who you are and what you are. Does everyone have the same disease? Does everyone have the same lack? Does everyone have the same need? No.

The listener, who sits in stunned silence trying to reconcile this knowledge to what they were taught when they were going to Sunday school, sits there and part of them knows it is the truth. They know it. Yet there is this other part of them that is trying to rationalize the knowledge. Rationalize means to judge it, to come up with a judgment about the information. When you learn about those two aspects of yourself, what part of you wants to rush to deny that which is clearly a compliment in the highest and loftiest realm?

Why would you want to deny that you possibly could be a Spirit intransient, that you possibly could be more than your body, that you possibly could be more than what you have worked for all your life? Why would you want to deny that? Why would you not want to even consider it? To deny that God lives within you is to deny your ability for unlimited knowingness, unlimited love, unlimited power, your ability to manifest what was called in elder times the kingdom of heaven. In the beginning I told people who came to see me this truth that was outrageous.

"Well, I can't possibly wake up tomorrow morning and say that I am God."

"Why not? Why can't you do that?"

"Well, someone may hear me."

"So what?"

"They would think that I had gone off the deep end."

"You have. That is the point."

This message I brought because this is what I learned in my life. Life is not about dying. I want you to know that. And life is not about living as an ascetic somewhere, trying to see only as God, because when you try to do that you remain separated. Life and God are interchangeable. They are, as it were, the same thing. So these people then started to say, "Well, so I am God," and they choked up. Then I taught them how to do wonderful things, and they were able to do wonderful things. And I said to them, now who did this? It was not I. Who did this in you? It was the God within you who did it. It is easy.

Now that is how I became famous and infamous here because I told you the truth. And what does it mean to know that? It means that there is a part of yourself you have never tapped into, and this has nothing to do with all of that hocus-pocus metaphysical garbage. This is not New Age. This is old age.

Your brain is a testament that you do not know everything. Do you know you use less than a tenth of that brain? What is the rest of it waiting there for, those empty rooms? It is waiting for something. Not even Einstein used the capacity of his brain. What could it be waiting for? It is waiting for this part of you who has not seen yet your better days, that part of you that knows everything that your altered ego insists you do not. It is waking up and realizing it and being outrageous enough to learn to say, "I know there is something greater to me. I have felt its movement, but I do not know how to access it. I do not know how to put my doubts aside. Indeed I do not know how to put my rational mind aside." So I say to you, what has your rational mind gained you? It has gained you retirement. It has gained you a good job. But it hasn't held your relationships together, and it has not prevented you from dying. And the rational mind also didn't cure your body when it was sick. There are some things that transcend that.

It is one thing to say you are God — it sounds really wonderful — but you are going to walk out and forget about that because it doesn't work in the marketplace. That is only a philosophy. But what if I taught you how to be one? What if I knew how to open up your brain and incorporate thought and manifest reality? Then we could say, was this the rational self that did this? Never. It is the irrational self because God is unlimited, which means you are too.

Students, particularly in this time, learn everything in school but fail to realize that everything they learn is theory. They go out in the world and then they endeavor to put that into practice. Imagine a computer scientist flipping burgers. It is difficult to put that into labor. So everything I am telling you today is not the truth. It is philosophy. It is my truth because I became it, earned it, and was it.

When will it become your truth? When will you know what I have told you will work? When you are able to do something that you could never do before. Then you will know truth. And if that is the only part of truth you picked up from this, it is going to be worth it all because it is a little seed that says, "I have the ability to do the remarkable, and God is not gifted people above me." There is no such thing as a gifted person. There are only those who choose to know and those who do not choose to know.

I have been able to maintain this truth that you are God for all these years without being ousted. It has been nothing in time for me. Do you know how many people have come and listened, have learned and been trained, and are now living it in the world? Many, thank God. It is not that they are a follower of me. Where are they going to go when I leave here? How could you follow Ramtha? You cannot follow me. It is impossible. Followers never learn anything. Students always learn. A student is willing to learn and be tested. Followers are never tested. They never learn. And of course the guru doesn't know anything anyway, so he is not going to teach them anything.

There are many entities in which this is a truth. You can't look at them and say, "That is impossible. How do you know God is within you?" You can't look at them and devalue them because they are outrageous, because they have touched something within themselves that has always been there. And what do they call that? They don't call it a name. They call it the Mother/Father Principle. "It is my Holy Spirit. It is the God within me. It is that which I ultimately am. And I am greater than my limitations." Now they know a truth. You don't yet.

I am still here teaching because regardless of what the world says, it is going to die, and regardless of how people think out there, they are not prepared for change. I am here not to change the world but to bring about, in individuals' lives who wish to know, a handful of masters. That is all. Those masters are common people who woke up one morning and said, "There is something more to life and I am missing it." These are the people who didn't quit their jobs, kick the cat, or leave their wife. These are individuals who say, "It is not the job of my wife, my cat, and where I live to make me happy. It is my job to do that. There must be something more." And these are the entities who come to learn.

They learn everything about themselves: their brain and how it works, their body and how it works, their dreams and what they are, and physics, how reality is created from the mind. They learn it all, and they go back and implement that into their lives. That is what I am here to do. When I have a group of people who can create reality out of nothing in a matter of moments in their hands, who can heal the sick with one touch, who indeed can do the remarkable, then all of this will have been worth it because they become then lights to the whole world.

They are common people. You are common people. And we are almost there. We already have entities that can do these things, and don't you think they were skeptical? They were all skeptical. It is easy to be that way. What is hard is to accept. It is easy to die. Those people that are killing themselves and thinking they are going to go on to a new life, rubbish. It is easy to die. It is hard to live, and yet that is the gift of God.

CONSCIOUSNESS AND ENERGY CREATES THE NATURE OF REALITY

Consciousness and energy creates the nature of reality. How many of you know what that means? What you think, you are, and what you think, your life is. How does that sound? That is pretty correct, but it sounds a little New Agey, doesn't it?

Consciousness is a fairly new term. It wasn't around in my day. It is a mysterious term because it can be just about anything that any writer wants it to be. It is a word that is an enigma because it struggles to explain self-awareness, it struggles to explain Spirit, it struggles to explain mind, and it struggles to explain self. Watching everyone struggle with this word is really beautiful. The word is a gift. Anyone who wants to use it can, without someone saying that is incorrect, because its definition has never truly been understood.

In the beginning all you were was consciousness and energy, which is everything there is. In this context, what does it mean? It means you are consciousness, which means awareness, which means Spirit. It means that you, the traveler with a soul — consciousness and energy with its scribe, the soul — have lived multitudinous lifetimes in many incarnations and in many bodies. The soul is that which is termed the scribe of all of your lifetimes. If you are consciousness, which means you are aware, and energy, which means you are mobile, if you were everything in the beginning why would you be down here in the murk and the mire of the plane of demonstration? What is the purpose of this life? To gain mind.

Now mind is another one of those words, isn't it? It is often confused with the brain. "My mind has a headache." Well, your mind isn't your brain. It is often confused as consciousness, but it isn't. Consciousness and energy is its parent. But what mind is, is the sum total of making known the unknown.

So in the beginning you are consciousness and energy, radiant being in the Void, one vast nothing, but you are aware of nothing. If nothing was all that you were ever aware of, it would be a common place. But the common place said to you, "Go and make known the unknown. Find out who I am, what I am." And you said, "Fine, I shall do that. Where do I start?"

"Well, start with start."

Contemplate what that means. Now here is where mind is created. When consciousness and energy contemplates the word "start," there is no reference for what the word means, but what it did do was the act of contemplation. Contemplation in consciousness and energy is a moving into, so when you move into and contemplate the word start — which you have no idea what it means — the act of contemplating must be the definitive definition of start, and it is. Consciousness and energy has now got a mind and the mind is made up of "start." How can the Void, one vast nothing, also have a mind? Our journey is to make known the unknown, and every act of creating something out of nothing produces a mind, a memory.

How long have you been doing this? Approximately ten and a half million years. You have been alive for ten and a half million years on this plane, on this earth, reincarnating, every incarnation into a new body. Why would the Spirit even need a body? Because this plane is heavier than consciousness and energy. It is the product of it. This plane is a mind. Why would you want to come down here? To make known the unknown, because you have never been here before. Ten and a half million years ago you fell into this plane. It is called materiality, and you are the creators of it. The purpose then of being lost into materiality is making it known, and if the only entity you have to make it known to is you, that is all that is sufficient.

Mind then is the prize of a lifetime. How then do we get from being consciousness and energy to processing mind?

What is mind made up of? Mind is made up of thought. Mind is composed of thought. Now that is another confusing word, isn't it? Do you really know what a thought is? You think about it sometimes but you never give it another thought. You never understand the mechanisms when you tell someone, "I have been thinking about you." What is thinking and thought? You do it all the time. You speak as if you are an expert on it, but you are not.

The Difference between Consciousness, Energy, Mind, Thought, and the Brain

What is the difference between consciousness, energy, mind, thought, and — somewhere we are about to throw in this creature — the brain? Perhaps you thought that thought was thinking and that thinking is self-awareness. "That is what consciousness is. Consciousness is thinking and I think also that consciousness is mind too." Well, that isn't the way that it works. A thought is a frozen moment, a memory of consciousness. If we saw consciousness and energy as a stream, then the brain has the capacity to photograph sections of that stream and freeze them. That moment of photography is called thought.

Consciousness and energy is what you are. Mind is the mission. Thoughts make up the mind. Then what is the mechanism in-between, and is mind localized? Mind is not localized. Consciousness and energy, inextricably combined, is everything. Its potential is everything and "everything," as potential, defines it, but its journey is to create from what it is. The act of creating produces a mind, and that is what we give to what we call the mind of God.

You would think that in ten and a half million years you would know a lot. Well, you do. This is called the first plane, and this is the body mass required for this plane. Every level has its body. Every level has its brain. In other words, think of this. There are seven heavens, which means there are seven levels which you can appear upon, and they are all determined by time. So within this room we have six other levels at work. You can't go to every one of those levels unless you have a body to be there, because otherwise you would not be able to participate in that level. Just for you to understand, all of you have bodies in the other levels, and this is the body that you currently have.

We created this place and we created time. The rate at which everything here vibrates is very slow. In order for us to continue to mold mind we must inhabit a body that is alien to what we are. I want you to understand that. The Spirit that you are is not this body, although the Spirit made this body. This body is the garment that we wear in this lifetime and it is beautiful because it is the most magnificent machine that was ever created and will never be duplicated. Why did we do that? Because in order for consciousness and energy to have tangible interaction with this planet and this time, we must inhabit a vehicle that vibrates at the same rate as this chair does, and so now you do.

Why then must we go to all of this trouble? To get this brain, your greatest possession in this body. Just think of it this way. All of you who are worried about your faces — how beautiful they are, how ugly they are — be grateful that this brain is this big because otherwise what would you hang it on? If in reality this brain was only as big as what you activate, then part of your eyebrows and eyes would be falling down on your chest because it wouldn't be very big. This brain is our greatest possession.

The complete mind of God — that means all of your lifetimes, plus all of the lifetimes of every bacteria that was ever created, every entity that was ever created, anything that produced a mind — is called the mind of God. Isn't it interesting that you were taught that the mind of God was composed of the mind of angels? Angels are stupid. That would not be a very wise God. The mind of God is not just about human beings either. It is about every bird that ever lived. It is about every virus that ever lived. Every tree produces mind. Now that is what we call the mind of God. So do you have it? All of you do. It sits right here in the lower cerebellum, the reptilian brain. The name of that part of the brain is the lower cerebellum. It is the seat of the subconscious and the mind of God.

How Is Mind Developed from Early Childhood

All of us, you and I, incarnated here, and we helped create this body and made the body self-perpetuating. We did that, and that is in the mind of God. This body is part of the mind of God. But the reason that this becomes so important to us is because the human brain is a biocomputer. It is a compelling statement, but it is. It is a computer because a stream of consciousness, which you are, surrounds the body and is always moving through this brain. Energy undulates. That is why it is called the serpent. Your consciousness and your energy hold this present body together. So your present body is continuously being affected by and bathed in a stream of consciousness, as well as prior mind.

We have to have something that that energy can move through that was created specifically to fire and receive high levels of subtle energy and be able to be so subtle to pick it up and transfer that energy into electrical firing at a very minute place in the brain. The stream of consciousness flows always from the lower cerebellum up through the neocortex. The neocortex is the new brain. It is the ignorant brain. You are just starting. In this school we call that the yellow brain. It is the new brain born with this physical body in this lifetime.

Now this brain back here, the lower cerebellum, is an amazing entity because it is passed on through every genetic line and it doesn't change. Your physicians call this the old reptilian brain. Let me tell you how beautiful this brain is. If you were to take a little razor and scrape just a wee bit off this brain — enough that you could put it underneath your fingernail — and put it under one of your microscopes, you would learn something incredibly amazing. You would find that that little scraping has more nerve cells interconnected than the entire yellow brain put together. It is very granular and very compact. Every time that you copulate and bring forth children in the fruit of the womb, it is programmed that every body will have that brain. It is inherited in every generation so that the mind of God, and you coming into that body with all of your knowledge, is carried with you. That is why when you learn to tap the subconscious, you are tapping the mind of God. This knows exactly why you are here. It knows your agenda here and why you are back in this body.

The neocortex doesn't know anything other than what the environment has taught it. It is our computer and it is with this computer that we freeze, in time, ourself. How does that work? The frontal lobe, your forehead, is often referred to as the third eye, and it is a little confused that the seat of the soul is connected to the pineal gland. The reason that the frontal lobe is so important is because whatever thought rests there becomes reality itself.

From the time you were ushered forth from the womb, you had about a year to decide whether or not you wanted to keep this body. After a year we assume that it is a yes. Most children start getting very smart at about four months, particularly past the first year because that means that its Spirit has decided to keep the body.

The learning after a year becomes very rapid. The Spirit, that which you are, just rests, and all the child does is being taught by its sensual body, meaning eyes, nose, mouth, hearing, touch. Everything is defined literally by the face itself because the child's job is to build up memory of the environment in the brain. Children learn very, very fast. If the child is fortunate enough to have a great parent who unlimits the mind of the child and allows the child to perceive the environment, then we have what we call a genius on our hands. If the parent, however, determines the environment, then we have just a duplicate of mother or father or the baby-sitter on our hands here.

Everything the child sees, smells, tastes, and feels is

logged in the brain by what is called a neuronet. The senses in the body have a neuronet base in the brain. The brain is made up of nerve cells, billions of them. They are the guts of the computer. The Spirit allows the child to develop that neuronet, and neurons move around a lot in the brain so it is possible to change your mind.

The Spirit does not take hold of the body until this is set into motion. This is what I mean. Children rarely create reality until their spiritual self has been activated, because youth is about putting together neurons in the form of memory in the brain. Children interact. They don't create; they interact. They go to school. Someone tells them what to do. They memorize it. Every day they participate in life. They don't create it. Now why is it that the spiritual doesn't happen until a certain time that you, as Spirit, decide to activate the brain? Because we are here to create reality and reality's creation develops mind.

Think about this for a moment. It takes over ten thousand neurons to activate and fire the color yellow in your brain. Just think of yellow for a moment, something yellow. Right now you have approximately ten thousand and thirty-five neurons firing in your brain to give you the color yellow. How do you see it? Are you seeing yellow with your eye? Are you seeing it with your visual cortex? How do you see yellow? How did you learn that as a child? You saw the color of a flower, and someone kept telling you that flowers are flowers but certain colors make certain flowers, and you were able to decipher that. Your first memories are of color, and that is why you have an eye, to be able to filter the hue to the brain so that it makes a connection.

Once we get yellow, we work on red, and then from red to green. There are many of you that when you were children thought that grass was the color yellow until someone kept telling you, "No, it is green." And when they kept telling you that, then you started to separate that grass isn't yellow unless there is a drought. This is how learning happens. In all your young life you were explorers. That is what youth is supposed to do, explore and learn a great deal until such time when there is a morning of maturity that occurs.

This makes some logic, doesn't it, because it would also begin to explain problems with reincarnation. It has always been argued that if you lived before, how come you can't remember? Furthermore, if you lived before and were an able-bodied woman, why did it take you so long to walk in this life? And how come you didn't know things? How come you still don't know things? Because this brain belongs to this life. The last lifetime had its own brain. This is a new life and it means you get to start over.

The Spirit knows everything. It knows all of this. It is bringing the brain into a state of technical and time maturity. What children know today, children fifty years ago did not know. If you lived fifty years ago and died, you would want to be reborn today because the advances in mind have been extraordinary in fifty years, and that is what you are after here.

So now you know how to read and write. You know how to do numbers. You know color. Your mind has been developed towards the arts. You know how to create sound. You know how to communicate. And then you have your little prejudices peppered through all of that, some of which have been your parents'. Now that you know a lot, the Spirit then wakes up.

FIG. 1: NEURONS FIRING AND THE SYNAPTIC CLEFT

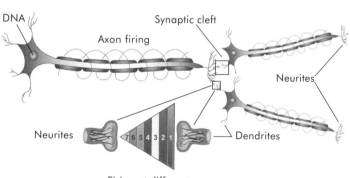

Firing at different
levels of quantum potential

In the brain you have billions of these neurons. They are massive, complex, and ingenious. The synaptic cleft is the place where the information is coming in. The Spirit knows when the brain is ready, that who you thought was you is now ready for enlightenment. It moves in and it reverse-fires the brain, which means that now the flow of energy around your body can start to move through the brain and the brain will start to fire and isolate that stream. Let's imagine that a stream of consciousness is long and the brain is going to cut it into very small pieces and arrange it, attach it to what is already known or move it in the brain. The brain is now mapping the Spirit's consciousness.

The Spirit moves through and the brain starts firing. This is what some have called vision, enlightenment, inspiration. All of those come from the spiritual body. They do not come from the yellow brain. The Spirit moves through a stream of consciousness and the brain freezes and maps it.

What is the reason that we are here? You incarnated into this body and have an agenda from the Plane of Bliss. You have something to do here: the unfinished business and getting on with creating, making known the unknown. You can't go further making known the unknown until you finish your job from your last lifetime. So what will be the first stream that will be laid down? The unfinished business from the last lifetime. That is the first pass over the brain. The reason that is the first pass over the brain is because the body has to be oriented or destined to a place in which the body, containing the Spirit, can finish the business of its mother's and father's kingdom and interact. That is the first pass. When that is all done then we get to make known the unknown, that which we have never done.

We know then that the first pass is the unfinished business from the last lifetime and that this brain of yours is starting to photograph every part of that because the brain, as a computer, creates holograms. Thought has more dimension than the person sitting next to you. Every thought that the child's brain makes is holographic and very visual.

The brain produces then a series of holograms, which we call thinking, created to flash in what is called the frontal lobe by the entire brain. Thinking is nothing more than the successive firing of holograms. Isn't it interesting that the brain doesn't think in language? The only language the computer knows is symbolism and that has been artfully created by the brain itself. There is a whole language center in the brain that deciphers the pictures into words that the body has to articulate.

FIG. 2: HOLOGRAPHIC EVOLUTION OF WRITTEN LANGUAGE

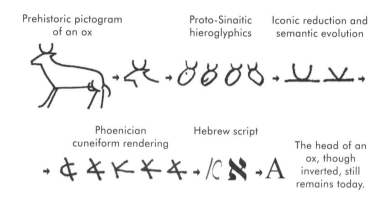

Prehistoric pictogram of an ox   Proto-Sinaitic hieroglyphics   Iconic reduction and semantic evolution

Phoenician cuneiform rendering   Hebrew script   The head of an ox, though inverted, still remains today.

The brain is a computer. Someone has got to be the programmer. That means someone has got to be home. Thought is holographic and is produced by a neuronet that represents forms. For example, the same neuronet that produces yellow can combine itself with the neuronet "round" and the neuronet "radiance," and when those three fire we have the sun. We can take the neuronet yellow, ten thousand and some neurons, combine it with a half-moon, and add a little shading. So far, now we have three sets of the brain firing because the moment that we add the shape to it, it kicks something else in. It kicks in a neuronet based in chemical taste. That kicks in and fairly soon the yellow has transferred into a banana. Delicious. Yellow both warms and is edible. To the brain that is how it works. We can take and put that in every part of life, that everything you have learned can be changed, mixed around, and produce different pictures. Nothing is absolute.

Thought is a hologram. Why would we go to so much trouble to produce a hologram that we already know exists? Because in this brain it presents its picture in the frontal lobe. That whole process is called consciousness and energy. That is the process in the body, because if we hold that hologram up here in the frontal lobe and let nothing else interfere with it, we are holding, by will, a thought. That desire to hold a thought is indigenous in us because something happens when we do that. That thought, bathed in the field of undulating energy at different frequencies that surround your body and are interconnected with all other energies, collapses all of this energy into particles.

THE STUDY OF ENERGY

Now we are going to study energy. Where does solidity come in? Way back then when we all started, there was nothing solid. Solidity is superficial. It is really an illusion. You think it is everything — and you are supposed to think that way — but the Spirit doesn't think that way. The reason why we have a body is because the body is determined to insist on solidity, to see the realism of something because it wants to taste it, smell it, see it, and feel it. That is what it is supposed to do.

Now look all around you and perceive the emptiness in the room. What about the empty space? What is occupying that space? Energy. And the things that you see are collapsed energy, including your body.

Fig. 3: Energy As a Wave and a Particle

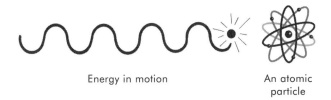

Energy in motion

An atomic
particle

Nothing exists outside of the primal cause, which is consciousness and energy. Nothing exists outside of it. It is the action on nothingness. That would suggest then that all power, all mind, all ability are self-contained in it, and they are. We could look at this wave drawing and say "that is me" and not be incorrect because this wave frequency is energy.

All energy is waiting to be formed. Everything around you has already been worked out and to go back and keep working it is sort of a boring task. What is adventurous is the space between you and me that you haven't worked out. It is this energy. This means that there is a raw field of potential that has not been thought about or acted upon.

Here is what quantum mechanics tells you — and all of you who want to understand how to manipulate energy should study quantum mechanics — that there is no such thing as solid matter. That is correct. The only way it became solid is that energy got collapsed, something collapsed it into a particle.

The Uncertainty Principle and the Observer Effect

Waves of energy are both active waves and particles. They are the same thing. Particles and energy are the same thing. What mysterious something determined that this free-flowing entity should suddenly wind up into mass? What causes energy to collapse into particle form is the Observer. That is what science tells you, the Observer. Well, who is that? It is you. In scientific tests — this is how unenlightened the scientists were — they were determined to prove that energy and particles were the same thing. They set up little tests and exactly what they thought it would do, it did. They thought they were geniuses. They did the tests again and again and again, and it did it. They go, "Ha, you see, I told you, energy is a particle. There is no difference."

Newtonian physicists, they come in with their doubt because they can't understand how that could be. For them, it is just a straight line and it ends somewhere. So they set up the same experiment, except do you know what they determined that the action would be? They came into the test with a predetermined thought, that it would react and behave according to the uncertainty principle. Well, it did.

And they did it again and said, "See, it has nothing to do with it being mass. Mass and energy waves are two separate things." And the other team came in and did the same test and it became energy into mass.

Here is what happened to a few ingenious scientists. They realized something, that energy behaved exactly according to the Observer observing the field. In other words, what they thought it would do, it always did. So everybody was right. The old classical physics, it is right, and the new enlightened physics, it is right too. Don't we have room for everyone's truth? This is wonderful news unless, of course, you are classical.

Let me show you how conscious light photons are. They did another little test. They didn't even want the light to hear them talk. They went into a leaded room and said, "This is what we are going to do. We are going to shoot a ray of light out but we are going to put a barrier in front of it. At the bottom we are going to put a little slit and on the back wall — we have a negative-sensitive wall — the moment light photons hit that wall we will be able to see them and map them because they will turn into a solid object at that point and leave their pattern behind." So once they agreed to this, they set up the experiment.

They actually had someone else set it up so as not to even inform the light what possibly was going to happen to it. They had another team turn on that wonderful ray of light photons. And here it goes, traveling, hits that wall, then climbs down, goes through the slit, comes out the other side, and leaves its print.

"Pretty smart, hmm?"

"You mean to tell me that light photons are conscious? Well, I'll be God."

"They certainly are."

If you don't believe me, have respect for science, believe them, because they showed that even when they sneaked behind light's back, light knew the game. It knew exactly what to do. Normally a ray of light would just hit a straight line, but these photon particles and waves went through the slit and onto the back wall. Don't you think then that the energy that exists between you and me is hyperintelligent? But if it is so intelligent, why does it need you? Because you are the Observer, you are God, and energy behaves to God.

You say, "Well, that is quite a stretch from the laboratory." No, it isn't. I could take you in there and you could observe a photon cloud and it would do exactly what you thought it would do. Then you would have to turn around and explain it to the scientist and he would understand and say, "Is that what you thought a photon cloud looked like?"

"Yep."

"Well, that is what you saw then."

FIG. 4: THE DOUBLE-SLIT EXPERIMENT

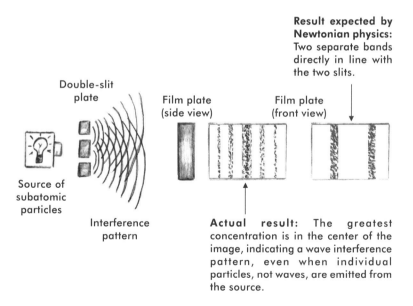

Source of subatomic particles

Double-slit plate

Interference pattern

Film plate (side view)

Film plate (front view)

Result expected by Newtonian physics: Two separate bands directly in line with the two slits.

Actual result: The greatest concentration is in the center of the image, indicating a wave interference pattern, even when individual particles, not waves, are emitted from the source.

Who is the Observer then in energy? You are. What is the force of observing? The hologram that sits right in your frontal lobe. This focus can do anything it wants to the energy field.

Here is something else I want you to understand. If that is the Observer, and it is, and this energy is already highly intelligent, then we would call the Observer the lord and energy the servant. We would call that consciousness and energy. All energy waves then have been something. When they collapse into particles it is because they have been focused into collapsing. That means that this whole wave will piggyback a pattern and collapse the pattern accordingly.

Understanding Atomic Particles

An atom is only one form that energy wears. Energy has created itself into every particle that ever existed. There is a conservation of energy in nature and it simply means that there are no set tachyons, and indeed there are no set light photons, and indeed there are no set electrons. Electrons have been nuclei, nuclei have been light photons, light photons have been tachyons — all particles. Why is this important for you to remember? For you as a student to know that you don't need to get more energy, you just have to recycle the energy you currently have. And you can have everything.

Having everything doesn't mean that you have to work out forty times a day to get energy. It doesn't mean that. It just means that the energy that is around your body right now that has held your mundane life into existence, mundane particles, can be traded in for outrageous particles and you don't have to do anything. You just have to re-form the holograms, and the moment you re-form the hologram as the Observer, your life will dissolve and re-form.

Do you understand, at least theoretically, that what you are thinking about affects the energy around you? Is it beginning to make a little more logic to you? And is it a little bit more believable? It is, isn't it? Well, that is called enlightenment.

WHAT IS REALITY?

Consciousness and energy creates the nature of reality. Well, what is reality? Your reality is composed of all the people, places, things, times, and events in your life. Your entire life is what you created it to be. You can't blame anyone else for participating in it. We are not victims; we are creators. That is our natural state of being. We are not victims. Now this is going to make some of you uncomfortable because you have all those hang-ups and guilts. You don't need to have any of it. Why do you still have it? Because you hold it into place and you think someone did something to you. They made you do it, or you did something to them, or you forced it on them. They succumbed and now you feel bad about it. All actions are self-determined. I want you to remember that. It is the most awesome, empowering statement you can say. And yet it takes an entity well-advanced to be able to say, "I created this mess. No one else did." Now that is hard to say, isn't it, because it is so much better to blame people instead of ourself.

Blame is one of the reasons you are caught on the wheel of reincarnation. You are coming back here because you have got to get it right. It is easy to point a finger to someone else and say, "It is your fault." That is an immature, walking-dead being. What is an enlightened being? This hurts, but to finally say, "I created this life and I take full responsibility for everything I have done and I lay not the blame any longer at anyone else's footsteps. It is me." Why is that liberating? Because in the same moment it shows how powerful you truly are. You are the Observers.

How do you want to wield the power of a master in life? The way that you wield the power of a master is to liberate your mind from blame and victimization, essentially the past itself. To be liberated is empowering because if you could have created this kind of suffering, if this life has been nothing but guilt, insecurity, fear, and shame, if you wasted a life doing that, that is where you as the Observer have held it all in orbit. What happens when you realize that? It all dissolves. Don't you know that the art of forgiveness is not asking someone to forgive you, it is to release them. Any true spiritual being will never tarry in a mind of guilt and shame. Those will be dealt with straightaway because knowledge turns the light on.

So what happens when you say, "I created this"? Think about this. What was the first pass of your Spirit when it came in? What did you have a propensity to do? Maybe the things that you did, you were supposed to do. Maybe that was the first pass. That is the unfinished business, and most of you have never even made it out from that first pass to taking care of it and moving on.

What happens when you suddenly say, "I did create my life"? Ah, there is something inside of you that twists and turns and has a vise on your soul that you just can't quite get it out because your pride is in your suffering. Arrogant people are those that suffer in pride, and pride won't let you give it up because it is a pet peeve. You will say, "Well, this is who I am." I will say to you, "That most certainly is, and you can have it. It is your creation." But what if you got over it and just flung it out there, what could possibly happen to you? A lot, because you never thought that way.

The Neuronet of the Personality

What is thought? Pictures. Where did the pictures come from? The brain. Does a brain have its own way of thinking? Yes, it is called personality. What is a personality? A personality is the sum total of neuronet programming. What is emotion? Emotion is the hormone reaction to that neuronet personality. What does that mean? That means that as a little child you were allowed to grow and to explore and to become — it is called the time of innocence — before a great maturity took you over. That maturity was the deep wisdom of your Spirit.

What happens is you have formulated a really rigid way of thinking. You haven't allowed your brain to mix it up yet. And who determines the mixing-up? It is you who do that, so you are really set in blame. But all blame is, is a neuronet. It doesn't exist anywhere out there. Where is your blame? Show me. I don't see it. It is in here in the brain. Why is it important to change the program? Because when you change the program you change the pictures. What happens when blame is let go and we shine the light of knowledge into this dark hole? Then we begin to think anew. The brain starts to react anew. The Spirit starts filling you with a feeling that feels right. The brain and reason argue with the feeling. Who do you go with, a set way of thinking or something that feels right? It has always been your choice.

What happens then if the light of reason and what you have learned here today abolishes your shame? How is your life going to change? This is the way it changes. You have held together people, places, things, times, and events in your life, everything you have done, by the personality. It holds it into place. How do we know that? Because those people, places, things, times, and events would not be in your life if first they were not in your brain.

So there is a continuous Observer. The brain personality is the cumulative Observer in the field of energy. Everything you can see in your life, every person that you know intimately in your life, everything you ever did in your life, the four walls that you call the hovel in your life, are all held together by the cumulative effect of the yellow brain's personality. That is who you are, all the way to the kinds of pictures you hang on the wall and your favorite colors. Your favorite colors are the predominant neuronet in the brain everything will be colored by. You cannot think without the brain. Thinking is the firing of a sequence of thoughts, and each thought is hooked up to a neuron. When they fire cumulatively, they produce a picture.

We can change the picture. We can turn yellow into a sun or into a banana. At will we can make the computer form the picture. Whatever we rest upon is what is causing reality out here to be held into place. How do we know that? You don't have to take my word for it. Go ask your scientists in quantum mechanics. Say to them, "What is the world really made out of?" and they will look at you and say, "Energy."

"How did this all get this way?" And they will say, "I beg your tolerance, but I can only speculate. It is our understanding that the world got this way through someone thinking it this way."

Change Expressed As the Love of Self

Why should your life be outside of science? Why should your problems be something that exist outside of this model? You are not that special. You are still a human being. So what happens if you give up shame? It is amazing. When that is given up in the brain, some part of your life is going to change almost immediately because the shame, fear, guilt, and lack are all held into place by a thought. Feeling is secondary. Emotion is secondary. Emotion cannot come unless it is first thought. What if we abolish it? Then there is no longer an Observer on a field creating the rebound effect of suffering, because if you did something to someone long ago or only yesterday and you feel the guilt of what you did, you will suffer because of guilt. You will have nothing to do anymore with that person because guilt becomes the primal thought process in the brain.

When we put together a thinking reality where you think "It is a beautiful day today," imagine the brain firing all those pictures. "It is a beautiful day today." It had to fire those pictures before it could even utter the words.

And then, "It is a beautiful day for everyone else but not for me. This is not my day. It never was my day." How about this? It undermines everything.

"Oh, you look so happy. Well, you should be happy. You have everything."

"Oh, I am. I am very happy. I am very happy. Aren't you?"

"I am glad you asked but, no, I have never been happy, and I have bought everything in the world that I could. I had all the money in the world and I had all of the people in the world. I have had all kinds of lovers. I have done all kinds of things. And I am still sitting here wondering what is it going to take."

I will tell you what it takes: Remove guilt that happened twenty-five years ago. Just remove it from your brain. When light is shined on it, the brain will see the logic of the teaching. And what do you put in its place? "I am a happy person." And when that can be spoken in the language of holographic forms, what happens to the unhappiness in your life and everyone that is connected to you in guilt? You all have this unspoken commitment. In order to have a sufferer, you must have a tyrant. So the brain creates a tyrant in your life that keeps you suffering.

This person that comes into your life doesn't know that they are there to make you suffer. This just happens to be a strong part of their character. There is nothing wrong with them. But with you it is everything because they make you suffer. They don't even have a clue they are doing that. That is the unspoken agreement. Good things happen to everyone but you. Pretty soon that is the agreement. No good thing comes your way.

"And I will never know love," and that is correct, that will be the agreement. You will never know love. No one will ever come into your life that will ever bring you love. Do you know why? Because love must first be fundamental to the self. What does that mean simply? You have to love who you are.

How do you do that? You take a look at your life and ask yourself, "Am I a sufferer? Do I regret? Am I a victim?

Am I filled with hate and rage?" You ask yourself that and if the answer is yes to any of those, the greatest way you are going to get love is to love yourself enough to release it. How do you release it? You replace that neuronet, hook it up. Instead of "the sun," hook it up to "a banana." And when the brain, as the computer, has the programming right, that is what will always fire. That is true forgiveness and that is the act of self-love.

You love yourself. Never torture yourself. Love yourself. Never compare yourself to anyone else. There is not anyone else like you. You love yourself. Don't think love has to do with what you look like. Love has to do with everything of substance in you. So give yourself love. There is no one like you, so stop being like everyone else. Stop thinking the world owes you something. It doesn't owe you anything. You owe yourself. Love yourself to forgive people in your life. It is not that you just want them to be forgiven, it is you who want to be forgiven. That is loving yourself.

Now what happens when you work that way on yourself? The agreement changes. The people that now come into your life all share that common denominator and love who they are. They are roguishly independent. They think more of their mind than their bodies and they find substance in an evening wind and find love in nature. And if they can do that, they most certainly have love for you because you deserve it. You never get what you don't deserve in life.

I began this little talk to you because I want you to know that understanding your life does not have to mean the end of your happiness. Oftentimes it is the beginning of it. You have looked around to everybody to try to find joy. You know, you have married people and made them promise you that they were going to love you. How about you promising you that you are going to love you? Why in the world did you place that burden on someone else? No one is capable of doing that. There isn't even a master in the unseen that has the power to love for you. Why do you expect a mere mortal like yourself to be so responsible for loving you?

Finding happiness in other people is only looking for misery because they are all going to disappoint you, just like you have disappointed everyone. How many people were disappointed because you didn't turn out the way they thought you should or look the way they think you should? How many people have been disappointed or embarrassed by your crudeness or grossness? You disappoint people all the time. That is nothing new.

What I want to say to you that is so vitally important is when you do look at yourself honorably, you do yourself a great service. If you lose your joy and you become sad for a while — understanding this isn't a medical condition — it is moving back and endeavoring to have more knowledge come up for self, allowing the brain to change without the hysteria of emotion. That is why we seek the safe haven in the midbrain. That is what depression is.

Now is it ever too late for anyone? It never is too late. If you live this entire life in stupidity and ignorance and the last day of your life suddenly the sunrise becomes important to you, seeing the next day, the morning, then that morning you will have a communion with life and with nature that in the blindness of your youth and the retirement of your middle age you never looked at and never felt. And if that last morning you are one with those golden rods of light dancing on your windowpane and if you catch yourself in every moment being a part of that, when you expire that will be the most important day of your life. Then the life was well worth it.

If we are Gods, as I have told you, then we are endowed with the responsibility of acting like them. If we are Gods, it is up to no one to make us happy but ourself. If we are Gods, it is up to no one to give us love but ourself. When we do love that which we are, then the God reigns in us because God is a giver and not a taker. Then you can love unconditionally all people because you can love without the condition that they reciprocate. Why would you need reciprocation if it is already in you? This is ultimate freedom and this is ultimately how a master loves. And isn't it beautiful? You don't have to worry about loving people anymore if they are too thin, or they are too old, or they are too young, or the color of their skin isn't right, or their balance sheet is in the negative. All that disappears because the genuineness of what you are is already there, and it has room for everyone.

This is what we mean by unconditional love must be given to you first. In all that you have learned from our brief time together, I want you to know this is the most important teaching. Without that knowledge and indeed without the effort of applying it you may create phenomena in this school, because you all have the ability, but ultimately the phenomena is not going to make you happy. Like everything else, it will be commonplace and you will still feel empty inside.

The Observer Manifests both
Skepticism or Open-Mindedness

It is the dreaming brain, given permission by the Spirit, that has created the life to make known the unknown and to create mind. So everything that you can see in your life, taste, smell, and feel, you have manifested. That is the sum total of your mindful effort.

Why is it that some dreams don't come true? Based on this model, the Observer creates reality with what the Observer focuses upon. Why would some of your dreams not come true? This is very important because for those of you who are skeptical, you know where your skepticism comes from? Your skepticism comes from you knowing full well that life is very hard and real, is very difficult, and daydreaming is for idiots.

You only know the bottom line. Your skepticism has prevented the greater dreams from ever manifesting because the dream, whatever it is for you, is a dream made up of multitudinous dendrites in harmony. This dream has its own neuronet. It is just as alive in the brain as your arm is alive in your brain. The brain doesn't see any difference between your arm and your dream. Now who does? It is called the logic center. The logic center is the Antichrist because in this center everything is weighed whether it is good or bad, yes or no, higher or lower, past or future, black or white, all of those silly things. Logic is about judging.

What you have done is that you believe someone's lie, someone's reality. You borrowed their Observer and you put it in your brain. And what was their Observer? It is called an opinion. Their opinion said, "Well, dream on, because I don't believe in dreams. I believe you have to work every day for your daily bread. If you are a man, you have to work by the sweat of your brow and use your brain to unseat other men and always maintain power and control. If you are a woman, use your feminine prowess to keep the man in line who brings home the money so you can get what you want. You can never let your guard down." Well, that is called the school of good etiquette. It is opinion. But in the dreaming brain it is attached to a neuronet that says, "You are not real. My arm is real, but you are not real." So we have the dream but we have a censor connected to it.

So how does it appear in the brain? The dream comes on in the brain, and the moment you become utterly involved, surrender to it, there is a little voice inside of your head. The brain doesn't have a voice but it can mouth words and it knows how to think words because it has memorized them. So from its memory bank comes this little voice that says, "It is only a dream. It doesn't come true," or "You are not worthy of it. Get real." It is an opinion voice — that is all that it is — and when the dream appears, it has got a cancer on it because that dream has every right to affect energy fields as your arm does. Ask yourself, "Does my brain really know the difference?" Haven't you ever heard a great master say, "This is but an illusion"? Well, it is. Now everything you are capable of putting together, is. All you have to do is remove your doubt. If you hold doubt to it, you lose. Doubt just keeps the old, the common. If you remove doubt, what have you to lose? What you have to lose are the old dreams in place of the new one. That is all. How long can you hold this focus up here in the frontal lobe?

In order to do that, it is sort of like working on a computer, making an image stay on the computer, and then slowly changing the image but never turning the computer screen off. In the human body that is called focus. The human personality doesn't like to do that. The personality likes to fly around and reconnect its boundaries. The only aspect of you that has the power to hold the focus is the spiritual being that you really are, and it can make the focus stand still. The moment you become that focus you lose all sense of time, place, and being. Suddenly you forget you are in this room, you forget you are in this body, but suddenly you are what you are focusing upon. It is called analogical mind. The moment you hit analogical mind you have set, as the Observer, this dream into being.

Let's talk about belief and disbelief. Why should you disbelieve in anything? What is there to disbelieve in? Think about that for a moment. How about life after death? Well, that is a little nebulous. What does it gain you to not believe in anything? What does it gain you to be open-minded? Everything. What do you lose when you give up doubt? Control. Control is very powerful, and people who are powerful are very controlling people.

You have just begun to learn. And if you took all of this knowledge, if you find forgiveness isn't about asking anyone else but it is about asking yourself, if you are tired of being unhappy and make up your mind to be happy, then this day has served its purpose well. You will find also that you will become healthier and happier and younger. Unhappiness is a disease that always manifests in the body. If you look at your life and go, "My God, I did create all of this; why couldn't I have done better," what is better? You can only do what you know. It is just that no one ever told you this and anytime someone tried to, there was always someone there to ridicule it. No one ever gave you permission to dream. Furthermore, no one ever told you the science of it. No one ever gave you permission to change your life and to say that is good, because I want you to know that God is all about change.

What is stagnant in our life is boring. It has been lived. It has been done. It has been thought. It has been tasted, smelled, and felt. That is boring. That is stagnation to the Spirit. When you start to change, it is not about hurting anyone. It is about the liberation of yourself. When you change, the Observer up there changes in you and your whole life is going to go through a metamorphosis, and when it re-forms, it will reflect exactly your state of mind. You have nothing to lose by loving yourself, only the past.

What have you got to gain? I am going to teach you how to dream like a God, how to accept the dream and to love the dream, to know that whatsoever sits here in the frontal lobe is, and to know the difference between the personality and the Spirit when it thinks.

When the Student Is Ready, the Master Appears

There is nothing that I have taught you that is good or bad. Good or bad doesn't exist in the kingdom of God. Good or bad is a privileged decision that human beings make. Oftentimes everyone is so afraid of being bad that they are never good. What I have expressed to you today is my truth. I have been around for a very long time and I understand human nature. If you were very wise, you probably saw some ideas of your own self being pointed out here, and if it got a little uncomfortable, do not worry. Everyone was squirming. But that doesn't mean what I have taught you is bad. Understand that it is not a criticism or a condemnation.

When you don't know any better and everyone around you is doing it, it seems to be the right thing to do. The reason that you need a teacher — and not a teacher on this planet because they are always influenced by commerce and acceptability or the stars or something — is that when the student is ready, the master appears. He doesn't call you up on the telephone. He appears. You cannot know what happens after death, nor does anyone in your society know for sure. That is still up in the air. The jury is still out on that decision. There is no one on this plane qualified to tell you where you came from, where you are going back to, and what was your mission here because there is not anyone on this plane that has been there. They are still here. And that is where you get this ridiculous concept that the stars guide your life. If you give your power away to some twinkling thing in the Void, you have really got a problem. Well, you can say, "But it all worked out." Let me tell you why it worked out. Do you have a clue? What properties were involved to make it so? Consciousness and energy. I have to tell you that whatever you accepted in that frontal lobe is going to happen. Now all fortune-tellers are always correct. They are even correct when they are wrong. Do you know why they are correct when they are wrong? Because you believe them. They are always correct. It is called mental manipulation.

Don't let any government official tell you you are being brainwashed and don't let corporate America suggest that to you, because they are the greatest abusers there are. Yes, the truth is always suppressed from the populace because if they know the truth, the game is up. No one in control wants anyone to wake up. That is why this is called the plane of demonstration and that is why when you come back here you are in a prison. You have to fight your way out of giving your power away to a deck of cards, giving your power away to a pot of tea, giving your power away to a psychic, and oftentimes do it alone. You are the creator of reality. If you understand that, you are wise men and women. When you understand that, don't go pandering after someone asking them what is in store for you because they might just tell you what you want to hear.

Every doctor, if he or she is worth their salt, is a witch doctor. Someone has to lead you out of here. It has to be someone who has already been where you are trying to go. If they have been there, can describe it for you, can tell you how to go there, how to do it, how to be, if they lay down the footprints for you and if you follow those footprints accordingly, you are going to end up somewhere.

The reason every student of the Great Work needs a teacher and hierophant is because they don't know. They have yet to formulate the knowledge to know where they are going. They don't know how to open up the subconscious. Everyone thinks that you open up the subconscious with drugs. I have to tell you, if you have to resort to hallucinogenic drugs to know God, you are messing with the wrong people. God didn't make you so complicated that what God is cannot reveal itself to you. All you have to do is learn the secret of opening the door, and it is not about destroying your brain. I want you to know that.

Those stupid people who take all of those drugs are so scrambled in their neuronet. They sound like prophets because they don't make sense. That is what you do not want to do. To be what I am telling you to be is so natural in you. You just have to know how to do it. For that, you have to have knowledge, and the knowledge has to be all-encompassing. It must include your body and how it works, your brain and how it works, your environment and how it works, and your genetics and how it works. Then you learn about the secret place called the frontal lobe. Then you are going to wake up some morning totally alarmed because you will understand that everything you have just been thinking every day of your life has been manifesting. Those silly thoughts that you are thinking as you are boiling water are manifesting. Those thoughts that you are having at your computer are manifesting as common thought. "Oh, my God, what I just think naturally is what is keeping all this together. How do I think uncommonly common?"

I teach you how to do that.

— *Ramtha*

Epilogue by JZ Knight: How It All Started

"In other words, his whole point of focus is to come here and to teach you to be extraordinary."

My name is JZ Knight and I am the rightful owner of this body. Ramtha and I are two different people, two different beings. We have a common reality point and that is usually my body. Though we sort of look the same, we really don't look the same.

All of my life, ever since I was a little person, I have heard voices in my head and I have seen wonderful things that to me in my life were normal. I was fortunate enough to have a mother who was a very psychic human being and never condemned what it was that I was seeing. I had wonderful experiences all my life but the most important experience was that I had this deep and profound love for God and there was a part of me that understood what that was. Later in my life I went to church and I tried to understand God from the viewpoint of religious doctrine and had a lot of difficulty with that because it was sort of in conflict with what I felt and what I knew.

Ramtha has been a part of my life ever since I was born, but I didn't know who he was and I didn't know what he was, only that there was a wonderful force that walked with me, and when I was in trouble — and I had a lot of pain in my life growing up — that I always had extraordinary experiences with this being who would talk to me. I could hear him as clearly as I can hear you if we were to have a conversation. He helped me to understand a lot of things in my life that were beyond the normal scope of what someone would give someone as advice.

It wasn't until 1977 that he appeared to me in my kitchen on a Sunday afternoon as I was making pyramids with my husband. We were dehydrating food because we were into hiking and backpacking. As I put one of these ridiculous things on my head, at the other end of my kitchen this wonderful apparition appeared that was seven feet tall and glittery and beautiful and stark. You just don't expect at 2:30 in the afternoon that this is going to appear in your kitchen. No one is ever prepared for that. So Ramtha at that time really made his appearance known to me.

The first thing I said to him — and I don't know where this came from — was, "You are so beautiful. Who are you?" He has a smile like the sun. He is extraordinarily handsome. He said, "My name is Ramtha the Enlightened One and I have come to help you over the ditch." Being the simple person that I am, my immediate reaction was to look at the floor because I thought maybe something had happened to the floor, or the bomb was being dropped. I didn't know. From that day forward he became a constant in my life. And during the year of 1977 a lot of interesting things happened, to say the least. My two younger children at that time got to meet Ramtha and got to experience some incredible phenomena, as well as my husband.

Later that year, after teaching me and having some difficulty telling me what he was and me understanding, one day he said to me, "I am going to send you a runner that will bring you a set of books, and you read them because then you will know what I am." Those books were called the *Life and Teaching of the Masters of the Far East* (DeVorss & Co. Publishers, 1964). I read them and I began to understand that Ramtha was one of those beings, in a way, and that took me out of the are-you-the-devil-or-are-you-God sort of category that was plaguing me at the time.

After I got to understand him he spent long, long moments walking into my living room, all seven feet of this beautiful being, making himself comfortable on my couch, sitting down and talking to me and teaching me. What I didn't realize at that particular time was he already knew all the things I was going to ask and he already knew how to answer them, but I didn't know that he knew that.

Since 1977 he patiently dealt with me in a manner that

allowed me to question not his authenticity but things about myself as God, teaching me, catching me when I would get caught up in dogma or get caught up in limitation, catching me just in time and teaching me and walking me through that. And I always said, "You know, you are so patient. I think it is wonderful that you are so patient." And he would just smile and say that he is 35,000 years old, what else can you do in that period of time? It wasn't until about ten years ago that I realized that he already knew what I was going to ask and that is why he was so patient. But as the grand teacher that he is, he allowed me the opportunity to address these issues in myself. He had the grace to speak to me in a way that was not presumptuous but, as a true teacher, would allow me to come to realizations on my own.

Channeling Ramtha since late 1979 has been an experience. Ram is seven feet tall and he wears two robes that I have always seen him in. Even though they are the same robe, they are really beautiful so you never get tired of seeing them. The inner robe is snow white and goes all the way down to where I presume his feet are, and then he has an overrobe that is beautiful purple. You should understand that I have really looked at the material on these robes and it is not really material; it is sort of like light. And though the light has a transparency to them, there is an understanding that what he is wearing has a reality to it.

Ramtha's face is cinnamon-colored skin, and that is the best way I can describe it. It is not really brown and it is not really white and it is not really red. It is sort of a blending of that. He has very deep black eyes that can look into you, and you know you are being looked into. He has eyebrows that look like wings of a bird that come high on his brow. He has a very square jaw and a beautiful mouth, and when he smiles you know that you are in heaven. He has long, long hands and long fingers that he uses very eloquently to demonstrate his thought.

Imagine then after he taught me to get out of my body

by actually pulling me out, throwing me in the tunnel, hitting the wall of light and bouncing back — and realizing my kids were home from school and I just got through doing breakfast dishes — that getting used to missing time on this plane was really difficult. I didn't understand what I was doing and where I was going, so we had a lot of practice sessions. You have to understand that he did this to me at ten o'clock in the morning and when I came back off of the white wall it was 4:30. I had a real problem trying to adjust with the time that was missing here. So we had a long time with Ramtha teaching me how to do that, and it was fun and frolic and absolutely terrifying at moments. You can imagine if he walked up to you, yanked you right out of your body, threw you up to the ceiling and said, "Now what does that view look like?" and then throwing you in a tunnel — and perhaps the best way to describe it is it is a black hole into the next level — and being flung through this tunnel and hitting this white wall and having amnesia.

What he was getting me ready to do was to teach me something that I had already agreed to prior to this incarnation. My destiny in this life was not just to marry and to have children and to do well in life but to overcome the adversity to let what was previously planned happen, and that happening included an extraordinary consciousness, which he is.

Trying to dress my body for Ramtha was a joke. I didn't know what to do. The first time we had a channeling session I wore heels and a skirt. I thought I was going to church. So you can imagine, if you have a little time to study him, how he would appear dressed up in a business suit with heels on, which he never walked in in his life.

It is really difficult to talk to people and have them understand that I am not him, that we are two separate beings and that when you talk to me in this body, you are talking to me and not him. Sometimes over the past decade or so, that has been a great challenge to me in the public media because people don't understand how it is possible that a human being can be endowed with a divine mind and yet be separate from it.

I wanted you to know that although you see Ramtha out here in my body, it is my body, but he doesn't look anything like this. His appearance in the body doesn't lessen the magnitude of who and what he is. You should also know that when we do talk, when you start asking me about things that he said, I may not have a clue what you are talking about because when I leave my body, I am gone to a whole other time and another place that I don't have cognizant memory of. And however long he spends with you, to me that will be maybe about five minutes or three minutes. And when I come back to my body, this whole time of this whole day has passed and I wasn't a part of it. I didn't hear what he said to you and I don't know what he did out here. When I come back, my body is exhausted. It is hard to get up the stairs sometimes to change my clothes and make myself more presentable for what the day is bringing me, or what is left of the day.

He has shown me a lot of wonderful things that I suppose people who have never gotten to see couldn't even dream of in their wildest dreams. I have seen the twenty-third universe and I have met extraordinary beings and I have seen life come and go. I have watched generations be born and live and pass in a matter of moments. I have been exposed to historical events to help me understand better what it was I needed to know. I have been allowed to walk beside my body in other lifetimes and watch how I was and who I was, and I have been allowed to see the other side of death. These are cherished and privileged opportunities that somewhere in my life I earned the right to have them. To speak of them to other people is, in a way, disenchanting because it is difficult to convey to people who have never been to those places what it is. I try my best as a storyteller to tell them and still fall short of it.

I also know that the reason that he works with his

students the way that he does is because Ramtha never wants to overshadow any of you. In other words, his whole point of focus is to come here and to teach you to be extraordinary. He already is. And it is not about him producing phenomena. If he told you he was going to send you runners, you are going to get them big time. It is not about him doing tricks in front of you. That is not what he is. Those are tools of an avatar that is still a guru that needs to be worshiped, and that is not the case with him.

So what will happen is he will teach you and cultivate you and allow you to create the phenomenon, and you will be able to do that. Then one day when you are able to manifest on cue and you are able to leave your body and you are able to love, when it is to the human interest impossible to do that, he will walk right out here in your life because you are ready to share what he is. And what he is is simply what you are going to become. Until then he is diligent, patient, all-knowing, and all-understanding of everything that we need to know in order to learn to be that.

The one thing I can say to you is that if you are interested in his presentation, and you are starting to love him even though you can't see him, that is a good sign because it means that what was important in you was your soul urging you to unfold in this lifetime. And it may be against your neuronet. Your personality can argue with you and debate with you, but that sort of logic is really transparent when the soul urges you onto an experience.

If this is what you want to do, you are going to have to exercise patience and focus and you are going to have to do the work. The work in the beginning is very hard, but if you have the tenacity to stay with it, then one day I can tell you that this teacher is going to turn you inside out. One day you will be able to do all the remarkable things that you have heard the masters in myth and legend have the capacity to do. You will be able to do them because that is the journey. And ultimately that ability is singularly the reality of a God awakening in human form.

Now that is my journey and it has been my journey all of my life. If it wasn't important and if it wasn't what it was, I certainly wouldn't be living in oblivion most of the year for the sake of having a few people come to have a New Age experience. This is far greater than a New Age experience. I should also say that it is far more important than the ability to meditate or the ability to do yoga. It is about changing consciousness all through our lives on every point and to be able to unhinge and unlimit our minds so that we can be all we can be.

You should also know what I have learned is that we can only demonstrate what we are capable of demonstrating. If you would say, well, what is blocking me from doing that, the only block that we have is our inability to surrender, to allow, and to support ourself even in the face of our own neuronet of doubt. If you can support yourself through doubt, then you will make the breakthrough because that is the only block that stands in your way. And one day you are going to do all these things and get to see all the things that I have seen and been allowed to see.

So I just wanted to come out here and show you that I exist, that I love what I do, and that I hope that you are learning from this teacher. And, more importantly, I hope you continue with it.

— *JZ Knight*

RAMTHA'S GLOSSARY

Analogical. Being analogical means living in the Now. It is the creative moment and is outside of time, the past, and the emotions.

Analogical mind. Analogical mind means one mind. It is the result of the alignment of primary consciousness and secondary consciousness, the Observer and the personality. The fourth, fifth, sixth, and seventh seals of the body are opened in this state of mind. The bands spin in opposite directions, like a wheel within a wheel, creating a powerful vortex that allows the thoughts held in the frontal lobe to coagulate and manifest.

Bands, the. The bands are the two sets of seven frequencies that surround the human body and hold it together. Each of the seven frequency layers of each band corresponds to the seven seals of seven levels of consciousness in the human body. The bands are the auric field that allow the processes of binary and analogical mind.

Binary mind. This term means two minds. It is the mind produced by accessing the knowledge of the human personality and the physical body without accessing our deep subconscious mind. Binary mind relies solely on the knowledge, perception, and thought processes of the neocortex and the first three seals. The fourth, fifth, sixth, and seventh seals remain closed in this state of mind.

Blue Body®. It is the body that belongs to the fourth plane of existence, the bridge consciousness, and the ultraviolet frequency band. The Blue Body® is the lord over the lightbody and the physical plane.

Blue Body® Dance. It is a discipline taught by Ramtha in which the students lift their conscious awareness to the consciousness of the fourth plane. This discipline allows the Blue Body® to be accessed and the fourth seal to be opened.

Blue Body® Healing. It is a discipline taught by Ramtha in which the students lift their conscious awareness to the consciousness of the fourth plane and the Blue Body® for the purpose of healing or changing the physical body.

Blue webs. The blue webs represent the basic structure at a subtle level of the physical body. It is the invisible skeletal structure of the physical realm vibrating at the level of ultraviolet frequency.

Body/mind consciousness. Body/mind consciousness is the consciousness that belongs to the physical plane and the human body.

Book of Life. Ramtha refers to the soul as the Book of Life, where the whole journey of involution and evolution of each individual is recorded in the form of wisdom.

C&E® = R. Consciousness and energy create the nature of reality.

C&E®. Abbreviation of Consciousness & Energy^{SM}. This is the service mark of the fundamental discipline of manifestation and the raising of consciousness taught in Ramtha's School of Enlightenment. Through this discipline the students learn to create an analogical state of mind, open up their higher seals, and create reality from the Void. A Beginning C&E® Workshop is the name of the Introductory Workshop for beginning students in which they learn the fundamental concepts and disciplines of Ramtha's teachings. The teachings of the Beginning C&E® Workshop can be found in *Ramtha, A Beginner's Guide to Creating Reality,* third ed. (Yelm: JZK Publishing, a division of JZK, Inc., 2004), and in *Ramtha, Creating Personal Reality*, Tape 380 ed. (Yelm: Ramtha Dialogues, 1998).

Christwalk. The Christwalk is a discipline designed by Ramtha in which the student learns to walk very slowly being acutely aware. In this discipline the students learn to manifest, with each step they take, the mind of a Christ.

Consciousness. Consciousness is the child who was born from the Void's contemplation of itself. It is the essence and fabric of all being. Everything that exists originated in consciousness and manifested outwardly through its handmaiden energy. A stream of consciousness refers to the continuum of the mind of God.

Consciousness and energy. Consciousness and energy are the dynamic force of creation and are inextricably combined. Everything that exists originated in consciousness and manifested through the modulation of its energy impact into mass.

Create Your Day^{SM}. This is the service mark for a technique created by Ramtha for raising consciousness and energy and intentionally creating a constructive plan of experiences and events for the day early in the morning before the start of the day. This technique is exclusively taught at Ramtha's School of Enlightenment.

Disciplines of the Great Work. Ramtha's School of Ancient Wisdom is dedicated to the Great Work. The disciplines of the Great Work practiced in Ramtha's School of Enlightenment are all designed in their entirety by Ramtha. These practices are powerful initiations where the student has the opportunity to apply and experience firsthand the teachings of Ramtha.

Emotional body. The emotional body is the collection of past emotions, attitudes, and electrochemical patterns that make up the brain's neuronet and define the human personality of an individual. Ramtha describes it as the seduction of the unenlightened. It is the reason for cyclical reincarnation.

Emotions. An emotion is the physical, biochemical effect of an experience. Emotions belong to the past, for they are the expression of experiences that are already known and mapped in the neuropathways of the brain.

Energy. Energy is the counterpart of consciousness. All consciousness carries with it a dynamic energy impact, radiation, or natural expression of itself. Likewise, all forms of energy carry with it a consciousness that defines it.

Enlightenment. Enlightenment is the full realization of the human person, the attainment of immortality, and unlimited mind. It is the result of raising the kundalini energy sitting at the base of the spine to the seventh seal that opens the dormant parts of the brain. When the energy penetrates the lower cerebellum and the midbrain, and the subconscious mind is opened, the individual experiences a blinding flash of light called enlightenment.

Evolution. Evolution is the journey back home from the slowest levels of frequency and mass to the highest levels of consciousness and Point Zero.

Fieldwork^{SM}. Fieldwork^{SM} is one of the fundamental disciplines of Ramtha's School of Enlightenment. The students are taught to create a symbol of something they want to know and experience and draw it on a paper card. These cards are placed with the blank side facing out on the fence rails of a large field. The students blindfold themselves and focus on their symbol, allowing their body to walk freely to find their card through the application of the law of consciousness and energy and analogical mind.

Fifth plane. The fifth plane of existence is the plane of superconsciousness and x-ray frequency. It is also known as the Golden Plane or paradise.

Fifth seal. This seal is the center of our spiritual body that connects us to the fifth plane. It is associated with the thyroid gland and with speaking and living the truth without dualism.

First plane. It refers to the material or physical plane. It is the plane of the image consciousness and Hertzian frequency. It is the slowest and densest form of coagulated consciousness and energy.

First seal. The first seal is associated with the reproductive organs, sexuality, and survival.

First three seals. The first three seals are the seals of sexuality, pain and suffering, and controlling power. These are the seals commonly at play in all of the complexities of the human drama.

Fourth plane. The fourth plane of existence is the realm of the bridge consciousness and ultraviolet frequency. This plane is described as the plane of Shiva, the destroyer of the old and creator of the new. In this plane, energy is not yet split into positive and negative polarity. Any lasting changes or healing of the physical body must be changed first at the level of the fourth plane and the Blue Body®. This plane is also called the Blue Plane, or the plane of Shiva.

Fourth seal. The fourth seal is associated with unconditional love and the thymus gland. When this seal is activated, a hormone is released that maintains the body in perfect health and stops the aging process.

God. Ramtha's teachings are an exposition of the statement, "You are God." Humanity is described as the forgotten Gods, divine beings by nature who have forgotten their heritage and true identity. It is precisely this statement that represents Ramtha's challenging message to our modern age, an age riddled with religious superstition and misconceptions about the divine and the true knowledge of wisdom.

God within. It is the Observer, the great self, the primary consciousness, the Spirit, the God within the human person.

God/man. The full realization of a human being.

God/woman. The full realization of a human being.

Gods. The Gods are technologically advanced beings from other star systems who came to Earth 455,000 years ago. These Gods manipulated the human race genetically, mixing and modifying our DNA with theirs. They are responsible for the evolution of the neocortex and used the human race as a subdued work force. Evidence of these events is recorded in the Sumerian tablets and artifacts. This term is also used to describe the true identity of humanity, the forgotten Gods.

Golden body. It is the body that belongs to the fifth plane, superconsciousness, and x-ray frequency.

Great Work. The Great Work is the practical application of the knowledge of the Schools of Ancient Wisdom. It refers to the disciplines by which the human person becomes enlightened and is transmuted into an immortal, divine being.

Grid^SM, The. This is the service mark for a technique created by Ramtha for raising consciousness and energy and intentionally tapping into the Zero Point Energy field and the fabric of reality through a mental visualization. This technique is exclusively taught at Ramtha's School of Enlightenment.

Hierophant. A hierophant is a master teacher who is able to manifest what they teach and initiate their students into such knowledge.

Hyperconsciousness. Hyperconsciousness is the consciousness of the sixth plane and gamma ray frequency.

Infinite Unknown. It is the frequency band of the seventh plane of existence and ultraconsciousness.

Involution. Involution is the journey from Point Zero and the seventh plane to the slowest and densest levels of frequency and mass.

JZ Knight. JZ Knight is the only person appointed by Ramtha to channel him. Ramtha refers to JZ as his beloved daughter. She was Ramaya, the eldest of the children given to Ramtha during his lifetime.

Kundalini. Kundalini energy is the life force of a person that descends from the higher seals to the base of the spine at puberty. It is a large packet of energy reserved for human evolution, commonly pictured as a coiled serpent that sits at the base of the spine. This energy is different from the energy coming out of the first three seals responsible for sexuality, pain and suffering, power, and victimization. It is commonly described as the sleeping serpent or the sleeping dragon. The journey of the kundalini energy to the crown of the head is called the journey of enlightenment. This journey takes place when this serpent wakes up and starts to split and dance around the spine, ionizing the spinal fluid and changing its molecular structure. This action causes the opening of the midbrain and the door to the subconscious mind.

Life force. The life force is the Father/Mother, the Spirit, the breath of life within the person that is the platform from which the person creates its illusions, imagination, and dreams.

Life review. It is the review of the previous incarnation that occurs when the person reaches the third plane after death. The person gets the opportunity to be the Observer, the actor, and the recipient of its own actions. The unresolved issues from that lifetime that emerge at the life or light review set the agenda for the next incarnation.

Light, the. The light refers to the third plane of existence.

Lightbody. It is the same as the radiant body. It is the body that belongs to the third plane of conscious awareness and the visible light frequency band.

List, the. The List is the discipline taught by Ramtha where the student gets to write a list of items they desire to know and experience and then learn to focus on it in an analogical state of consciousness. The List is the map used to design, change, and reprogram the neuronet of the person. It is the tool that helps to bring meaningful and lasting changes in the person and their reality.

Make known the unknown. This phrase expresses the original divine mandate given to the Source consciousness to manifest and bring to conscious awareness all of the infinite potentials of the Void. This statement represents the basic intent that inspires the dynamic process of creation and evolution.

Mind. Mind is the product of streams of consciousness and energy acting on the brain creating thought-forms, holographic segments, or neurosynaptic patterns called memory. The streams of consciousness and energy are what keep the brain alive. They are its power source. A person's ability to think is what gives them a mind.

Mind of God. The mind of God comprises the mind and wisdom of every lifeform that ever lived on any dimension, in any time, or that ever will live on any planet, any star, or region of space.

Mirror consciousness. When Point Zero imitated the act of contemplation of the Void it created a mirror reflection of itself, a point of reference that made the exploration of the Void possible. It is called mirror consciousness or secondary consciousness. See **Self.**

Monkey-mind. Monkey-mind refers to the flickering, swinging mind of the personality.

Mother/Father Principle. It is the source of all life, the Father, the eternal Mother, the Void. In Ramtha's teachings, the Source and God the creator are not the same. God the creator is seen as Point Zero and primary consciousness but not as the Source, or the Void, itself.

Name-field. The name-field is the name of the large field where the discipline of Fieldwork^SM is practiced.

Neighborhood Walk^SM. This is the service mark of a technique created by JZ Knight for raising consciousness and energy and intentionally modifying our neuronets and set patterns of thinking no longer wanted and replacing them with new ones of our choice. This technique is exclusively taught at Ramtha's School of Enlightenment.

Neuronet. The contraction for "neural network," a network of neurons that perform a function together.

Observer. It refers to the Observer responsible for collapsing the particle/wave of quantum mechanics. It represents the great self, the Spirit, primary consciousness, the God within the human person.

Outrageous. Ramtha uses this word in a positive way to express something or someone who is extraordinary and unusual, unrestrained in action, and excessively bold or fierce.

People, places, things, times, and events. These are the main areas of human experience to which the personality is emotionally attached. These areas represent the past of the human person and constitute the content of the emotional body.

Personality, the. See **Emotional body.**

Plane of Bliss. It refers to the plane of rest where souls get to plan their next incarnations after their life reviews. It is also known as heaven and paradise where there is no suffering, no pain, no need or lack, and where every wish is immediately manifested.

Plane of demonstration. The physical plane is also called the plane of demonstration. It is the plane where the person has the opportunity to demonstrate its creative potentiality in mass and witness consciousness in material form in order to expand its emotional understanding.

Point Zero. It refers to the original point of awareness created by the Void through its act of contemplating itself. Point Zero is the original child of the Void, the birth of consciousness.

Primary consciousness. It is the Observer, the great self, the God within the human person.

Ram. Ram is a shorter version of the name Ramtha. Ramtha means the Father.

Ramaya. Ramtha refers to JZ Knight as his beloved daughter. She was Ramaya, the first one to become Ramtha's adopted child during his lifetime. Ramtha found Ramaya abandoned on the steppes of Russia. Many people gave their children to Ramtha during the march as a gesture of love and highest respect; these children were to be raised in the House of the Ram. His children grew to the great number of 133 even though he never had offspring of his own blood.

Ramtha (etymology). The name of Ramtha the Enlightened One, Lord of the Wind, means the Father. It also refers to the Ram who descended from the mountain on what is known as the terrible day of the Ram. "It is about that in all antiquity. And in ancient Egypt, there is an avenue dedicated to the Ram, the great conqueror. And they were wise enough to understand that whoever could walk down the avenue of the Ram could conquer the wind." The word Aram, the name of Noah's grandson, is formed from the Aramaic noun Araa — meaning earth, landmass — and the word Ramtha, meaning high. This Semitic name echoes Ramtha's descent from the high mountain, which began the great march.

Runner. A runner in Ramtha's lifetime was responsible for bringing specific messages or information. A master teacher has the ability to send runners to other people that manifest their words or intent in the form of an experience or an event.

Second plane. It is the plane of existence of social consciousness and the infrared frequency band. It is associated with pain and suffering. This plane is the negative polarity of the third plane of visible light frequency.

Second seal. This seal is the energy center of social consciousness and the infrared frequency band. It is associated with the experience of pain and suffering and is located in the lower abdominal area.

Secondary consciousness. When Point Zero imitated the act of contemplation of the Void it created a mirror reflection of itself, a point of reference that made the exploration of the Void possible. It is called mirror consciousness or secondary consciousness. *See* **Self.**

Self, the. The self is the true identity of the human person different from the personality. It is the transcendental aspect of the person. It refers to the secondary consciousness, the traveler in a journey of involution and evolution making known the unknown.

Sending-and-receiving. Sending-and-receiving is the name of the discipline taught by Ramtha in which the student learns to access information using the faculties of the midbrain to the exclusion of sensory perception. This discipline develops the student's psychic ability of telepathy and divination.

Seven seals. The seven seals are powerful energy centers that constitute seven levels of consciousness in the human body. The bands are the way in which the physical body is held together according to these seals. In every human being there is energy spiraling out of the first three seals or centers. The energy pulsating out of the first three seals manifests itself respectively as sexuality, pain, or power. When the upper seals are unlocked, a higher level of awareness is activated.

Seventh plane. The seventh plane is the plane of ultraconsciousness and the Infinite Unknown frequency band. This plane is where the journey of involution began. This plane was created by Point Zero when it imitated the act of contemplation of the Void and the mirror or secondary consciousness was created. A plane of existence or dimension of space and time exists between two points of consciousness. All the other planes were created by slowing down the time and frequency band of the seventh plane.

Seventh seal. This seal is associated with the crown of the head, the pituitary gland, and the attainment of enlightenment.

Shiva. The Lord God Shiva represents the Lord of the Blue Plane and the Blue Body®. Shiva is not used in reference to a singular deity from Hinduism. It is rather the representation of a state of consciousness that belongs to the fourth plane, the ultraviolet frequency band, and the opening of the fourth seal. Shiva is neither male nor female. It is an androgynous being, for the energy of the fourth plane has not yet been split into positive and negative polarity. This is an important distinction from the traditional Hindu representation of Shiva as a male deity who has a wife. The tiger skin at its feet, the trident staff, and the sun and the moon at the level of the head represent the mastery of this body over the first three seals of consciousness. The kundalini energy is pictured as fiery energy shooting from the base of the spine through the head. This is another distinction from some Hindu representations of Shiva with the serpent energy coming out at the level of the fifth seal or throat. Another symbolic image of Shiva is the long threads of dark hair and an abundance of pearl necklaces, which represent its richness of experience owned into wisdom. The quiver and bow and arrows are the agent by which Shiva shoots its powerful will and destroys imperfection and creates the new.

Sixth plane. The sixth plane is the realm of hyperconsciousness and the gamma ray frequency band. In this plane the awareness of being one with the whole of life is experienced.

Sixth seal. This seal is associated with the pineal gland and the gamma ray frequency band. The reticular formation that filters and veils the knowingness of the subconscious mind is opened when this seal is activated. The opening of the brain refers to the opening of this seal and the activation of its consciousness and energy.

Social consciousness. It is the consciousness of the second plane and the infrared frequency band. It is also called the image of the human personality and the mind of the first three seals. Social consciousness refers to the collective consciousness of human society. It is the collection of thoughts, assumptions, judgments, prejudices, laws, morality, values, attitudes, ideals, and emotions of the fraternity of the human race.

Soul. Ramtha refers to the soul as the Book of Life, where the whole journey of involution and evolution of the individual is recorded in the form of wisdom.

Subconscious mind. The seat of the subconscious mind is the lower cerebellum or reptilian brain. This part of the brain has its own independent connections to the frontal lobe and the whole of the body and has the power to access the mind of God, the wisdom of the ages.

Superconsciousness. This is the consciousness of the fifth plane and the x-ray frequency band.

Tahumo. Tahumo is the discipline taught by Ramtha in which the student learns the ability to master the effects of the natural environment — cold and heat — on the human body.

Tank field. It is the name of the large field with the labyrinth that is used for the discipline of The Tank®.

Tank®, The. It is the name given to the labyrinth used as part of the disciplines of Ramtha's School of Enlightenment. The students are taught to find the entry to this labyrinth blindfolded and move through it focusing on the Void without touching the walls or using the eyes or the senses. The objective of this discipline is to find, blindfolded, the center of the labyrinth or a room designated and representative of the Void.

Third plane. This is the plane of conscious awareness and the visible light frequency band. It is also known as the light plane and the mental plane. When the energy of the Blue Plane is lowered down to this frequency band, it splits into positive and negative polarity. It is at this point that the soul splits into two, giving origin to the phenomenon of soulmates.

Third seal. This seal is the energy center of conscious awareness and the visible light frequency band. It is associated with control, tyranny, victimization, and power. It is located in the region of the solar plexus.

Thought. Thought is different from consciousness. The brain processes a stream of consciousness, modifying it into segments — holographic pictures — of neurological, electrical, and chemical prints called thoughts. Thoughts are the building blocks of mind.

Torsion Process[SM]. This is the service mark of a technique created by Ramtha for raising consciousness and energy and intentionally creating a torsion field using the mind. Through this technique the student learns to build a wormhole in space/time, alter reality, and create dimensional phenomena such as invisibility, levitation, bilocation, teleportation, and others. This technique is exclusively taught at Ramtha's School of Enlightenment.

Twilight®. This term is used to describe the discipline taught by Ramtha in which the students learn to put their bodies in a catatonic state similar to deep sleep, yet retaining their conscious awareness.

Twilight® Visualization Process. It is the process used to practice the discipline of the List or other visualization formats.

Ultraconsciousness. It is the consciousness of the seventh plane and the Infinite Unknown frequency band. It is the consciousness of an ascended master.

Unknown God. The Unknown God was the single God of Ramtha's ancestors, the Lemurians. The Unknown God also represents the forgotten divinity and divine origin of the human person.

Upper four seals. The upper four seals are the fourth, fifth, sixth, and seventh seals.

Void, the. The Void is defined as one vast nothing materially, yet all things potentially. *See* **Mother/Father Principle.**

Yellow brain. The yellow brain is Ramtha's name for the neocortex, the house of analytical and emotional thought. The reason why it is called the yellow brain is because the neocortices were colored yellow in the original two-dimensional, caricature-style drawing Ramtha used for his teaching on the function of the brain and its processes. He explained that the different aspects of the brain in this particular drawing are exaggerated and colorfully highlighted for the sake of study and understanding. This specific drawing became the standard tool used in all the subsequent teachings on the brain.

Yeshua ben Joseph. Ramtha refers to Jesus Christ by the name Yeshua ben Joseph, following the Jewish traditions of that time.

Fig. A: The Seven Seals:
Seven Levels of Consciousness in the Human Body

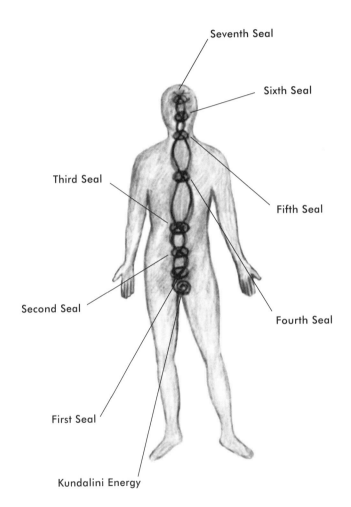

Copyright © 2000 JZ Knight

FIG. B: SEVEN LEVELS OF CONSCIOUSNESS AND ENERGY

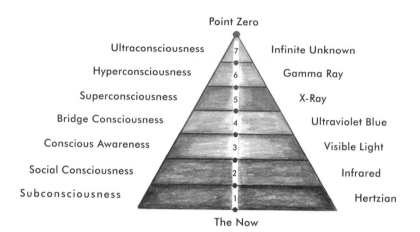

FIG. C: SEVEN BODIES ENFOLDED WITHIN EACH OTHER

Fig. D: Consciousness and Energy in the Light Spectrum

THE LIGHT SPECTRUM

CONSCIOUSNESS	ENERGY
Ultraconsciousness ⟷	Infinite Unknown
Hyperconsciousness ⟷	Gamma Ray
Superconsciousness ⟷	X-Ray
Bridge Consciousness ⟷	Ultraviolet Blue
Conscious Awareness ⟷	Visible Light
Social Consciousness ⟷	Infrared
Subconsciousness ⟷	Hertzian

TOP ◄

CENTER ◄

BOTTOM ◄

FIG. E: THE BRAIN

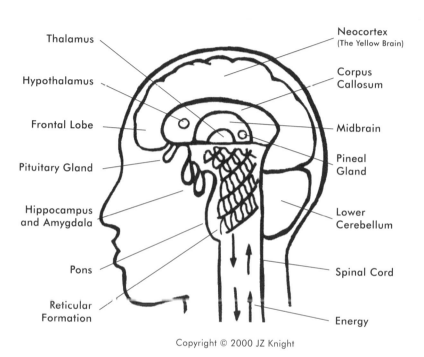

Thalamus

Hypothalamus

Frontal Lobe

Pituitary Gland

Hippocampus
and Amygdala

Pons

Reticular
Formation

Neocortex
(The Yellow Brain)

Corpus
Callosum

Midbrain

Pineal
Gland

Lower
Cerebellum

Spinal Cord

Energy

Copyright © 2000 JZ Knight

This is the original two-dimensional caricature-style drawing Ramtha used for his teaching on the function of the brain and its processes. He explained that the different aspects of the brain in this particular drawing are exaggerated and colorfully highlighted for the sake of study and understanding. This specific drawing became the standard tool used in all the subsequent teachings on the brain.

FIG. F: BINARY MIND — LIVING THE IMAGE

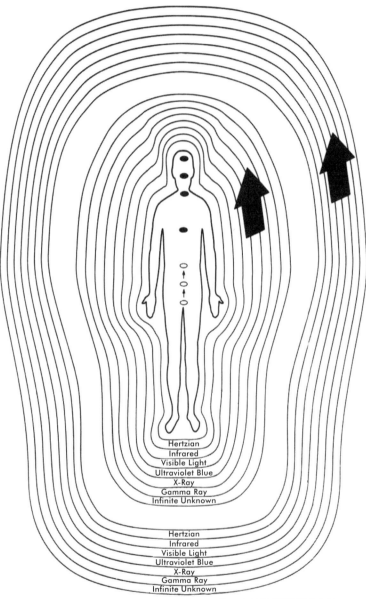

Hertzian
Infrared
Visible Light
Ultraviolet Blue
X-Ray
Gamma Ray
Infinite Unknown

Hertzian
Infrared
Visible Light
Ultraviolet Blue
X-Ray
Gamma Ray
Infinite Unknown

FIG. G: ANALOGICAL MIND — LIVING IN THE NOW

Hertzian
Infrared
Visible Light
Ultraviolet Blue
X-Ray
Gamma Ray
Infinite Unknown

Infinite Unknown
Infinite Unknown
Infinite Unknown
Infinite Unknown
Infinite Unknown
Infinite Unknown
Infinite Unknown

FIG. H: THE OBSERVER EFFECT AND THE NERVE CELL

The Observer is responsible
for collapsing the wave function of probability
into particle reality.

Particle   Energy wave   The Observer

The act of observation
makes the nerve cells fire and produces thought.

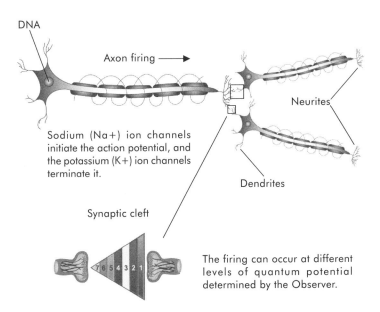

DNA

Axon firing ⟶

Neurites

Sodium (Na+) ion channels
initiate the action potential, and
the potassium (K+) ion channels
terminate it.

Dendrites

Synaptic cleft

The firing can occur at different
levels of quantum potential
determined by the Observer.

FIG. I: CELLULAR BIOLOGY AND THE THOUGHT CONNECTION

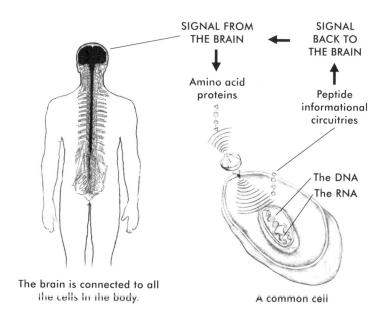

SIGNAL FROM
THE BRAIN

SIGNAL
BACK TO
THE BRAIN

Amino acid
proteins

Peptide
informational
circuitries

The DNA
The RNA

The brain is connected to all
the cells in the body.

A common cell

Copyright © 2000 JZ Knight

Fig. J: Weblike Skeletal Structure of Mass

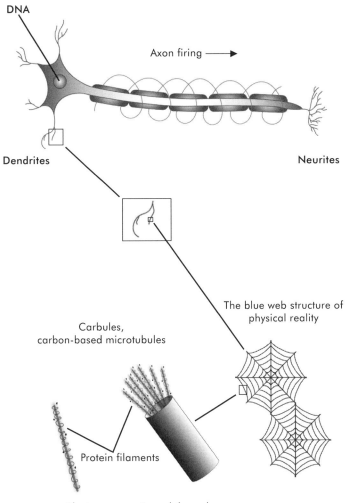

DNA

Axon firing ⟶

Dendrites

Neurites

The blue web structure of physical reality

Carbules, carbon-based microtubules

Protein filaments

Electrons move in and through the protein filaments.

Fig. K: The Blue Body®

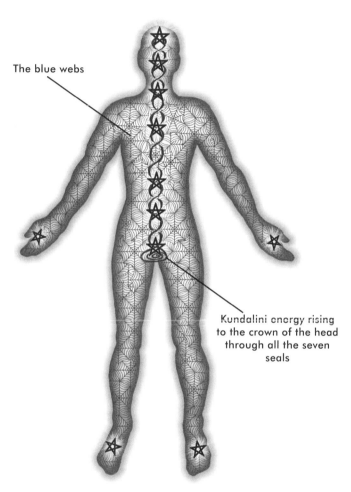

The blue webs

Kundalini energy rising
to the crown of the head
through all the seven
seals

Ramtha's School of Enlightenment
THE SCHOOL OF ANCIENT WISDOM

A Division of JZK, Inc.
P.O. Box 1210
Yelm, Washington 98597
360.458.5201
800.347.0439
www.ramtha.com
www.jzkpublishing.com